MON

Neal Bell
from the novel
Frankenstein
by Mary Shelley

BROADWAY PLAY PUBLISHING INC
224 E 62nd St, NY NY 10065-8201
212 772-8334 fax: 212 772-8358
BroadwayPlayPubl.com

MONSTER
© Copyright 2003 by Neal Bell

First printing: December 2003
This printing: December 2011
I S B N: 978-0-88145-228-0

Book design: Marie Donovan
Typeface: Palatino
Copy editing: Sue Gilad
Printed and bound in the U S A

ABOUT THE AUTHOR

Mr Bell's plays—including TWO SMALL BODIES, RAW YOUTH, COLD SWEAT, READY FOR THE RIVER, SLEEPING DOGS, RAGGED DICK, ON THE BUM, and SOMEWHERE IN THE PACIFIC—have appeared at Playwrights Horizons in New York and at regional theatres, including the Berkeley Rep, the Mark Taper Forum, South Coast Rep, the La Jolla Playhouse, and Actors Theater of Louisville, where his ten-minute play OUT THE WINDOW was a co-winner of the 1990 Heideman Award. Mr Bell has been a playwright-in-residence at the Yale Drama School and has taught playwriting at New York University, Playwrights Horizons Theater School, and the 42nd Street Collective. A recipient of fellowships from the Rockefeller Foundation, the National Endowment, and the Guggenheim Foundation, Mr Bell was awarded an Obie Award in 1992 for sustained achievement in playwriting.

Broadway Play Publishing Inc has published
McTEAGUE, RAGGED DICK, & THÉRÈSE RAQUIN
in a collection entitled PLAYS BY NEAL BELL.

MONSTER was first produced by Classic Stage Company (Barry Edelstein, Artistic Director), opening on 15 January 2002. The cast and creative contributors were:

WALTON . . . . Jonno Roberts
FORSTER . . . . Michael Cullen
VICTOR . . . . Jake Weber
FATHER . . . . Michael Cullen
MOTHER . . . . Christen Clifford
ELIZABETH . . . . Annie Parisse
CAT . . . . Michael Pitt
CLERVAL . . . . Jonno Roberts
JUSTINE . . . . Christen Clifford
WILLIAM . . . . Michael Pitt
CREATURE . . . . Christopher Donahue

Director . . . . Michael Greif
Set design . . . . Robert Brill
Costume design . . . . Jess Goldstein
Lighting design . . . . Kenneth Posner
Sound design . . . . Jane Shaw
Fight director . . . . J Steven White

CHARACTERS & SETTING

WALTON, *captain of the* Aurora
FORSTER, WALTON'*s first mate*
TWO DOGS
VICTOR, *a young doctor*
FATHER
MOTHER
ELIZABETH, VICTOR'*s cousin*
CAT
CLERVAL, VICTOR'*s friend*
JUSTINE, *a servant in* VICTOR'*s household*
WILLIAM, VICTOR'*s younger brother*
CREATURE, VICTOR'*s creation*

The early 1800s

Somewhere in the Arctic Ocean and Europe

NOTE

MONSTER can be performed with a cast of five men and two women, with the doubling of these characters:
FORSTER/FATHER
WALTON/CLERVAL
CAT/WILLIAM
JUSTINE/MOTHER

The parts of the barking but non-speaking DOGS can be doubled by available actors in Scenes Two and Four of ACT ONE.

Prop-note: The "Leyden jar", which appears in the thunderstorm scene in ACT ONE, is a metal-lined glass jar, with a metal rod sticking out of the lid.

ACT ONE

Scene One

(On board the ship Aurora. *Somewhere in the Arctic Ocean. The young captain* ROBERT WALTON *stands on the deck, looking out at the polar twilight.)*

(Lieutenant FORSTER, *an older man, approaches. He watches his captain anxiously, then finally speaks.)*

FORSTER: If we turn back now...

(He gets no response.)

FORSTER: Captain?

WALTON: *(Pointing out)*
What do you see?

FORSTER: The jaws of a trap.
And we're sailing into it.
Nothing but ice ahead of us—
one channel of open water behind.
And when *that* lane freezes up—

WALTON: *(Not disagreeing)*
I thought I could just make out...
against the sun—
what little sun there is, blood-red
and fading—almost gone...

(FORSTER regards his captain with concern.)

FORSTER: Sir?

WALTON: *(Pointing off)*
A team of dogs, crossing the ice...
and standing on the runners: a man...

(FORSTER, *nervous, looks out.*)

FORSTER: We're a hundred miles from land. More.

WALTON: Any land that *we* know of.
But what if the legends are true,
of a tropical valley—

FORSTER: At the North Pole?

WALTON: I've heard reports, of thermal springs—

FORSTER: Sailors lie. Or have you seen a mermaid,
lately?
I haven't. What I see is ice,
and dark closing in.
No man could live here.
(Pause)
We didn't find the Pole.
We found nothing, sir.
And our time has run out.

WALTON: *(Doubting his own sanity)*
Look again: you don't see a man
unharnessing his dogs?

FORSTER: *(Shaking his head)*
My father told me—
"No man goes to hell before his time."
Fair enough—but why did you decide
our time was now?
Eighteen men will die, unless you
give the order to come about.

WALTON: *(Peering out)*
But I can't be imagining this.
I even hear the dogs. Don't you?

*(For the first time, we hear the distant barking of dogs.
So—astonished—does* FORSTER. *But he's afraid to admit it.)*

FORSTER: No! Only the wind. Nothing is out there, sir.
(Seeing WALTON *ignoring him)*
WE FAILED!

WALTON: We didn't.
Isn't that why you're afraid?
Isn't that why I can smell the drizzly shit
running down your leg?
We were searching for the Unknown.
And now we've found it.
I have to get down to the ice.

*(*WALTON *rushes off, as* FORSTER *looks out, dismayed.)*

FORSTER: Then we've come to the end of the earth,
and my captain's insane—
*(Shouting a mock-courtesy, to the
offstage* WALTON)
begging your pardon, sir—
(To himself)
and we're all of us bloody well fucked—
because—I see him, too:
a man alone, in the twilight...
(Shouting off to the stranger:)
WHO ARE YOU?

Scene Two

(Adrift on an iceberg. VICTOR FRANKENSTEIN *faces his two
remaining* DOGS, *who keep their distance.)*

VICTOR: I thought you understood:
this is only a resting place—we have to go on.
If there's any game about,
it must be ahead of us, not behind.

(He takes a step in the DOGS' *direction. Baring fangs, they back away, growling.)*

VICTOR: No? I see: you've had enough.
But you *do* realize that you're starving?
A day ago, one of you stumbled and fell,
and the rest of you ate him.
Remember?
One of you I kicked away,
so I could tear at the carcass myself.
Why did you eat your fellow? Why did I?
To stay alive.
In the beginning was the Word.
What was the Word—"EAT"?

(Behind VICTOR, *at the far edge of the ice-floe,* WALTON *is clambering up.* VICTOR *doesn't sense his presence, at first—but the dogs go wild.)*

VICTOR: *(To the* DOGS*)*
Has he doubled back? Has he found me?
(Afraid to turn around)
In the Beginning—"Devour."

(Resigned, he sinks to his knees. In spite of their fear of the stranger WALTON, *the* DOGS *smell* VICTOR'S *weakness and begin to move closer, circling. Alarmed,* WALTON *draws a pistol and shouts at the* DOGS.*)*

WALTON: No! Get back! Get away from him!

(The DOGS *ignore him.* WALTON *shoots into the air, and the* DOGS, *snarling, lope away into the dark.* VICTOR *can't bring himself to face his savior.)*

VICTOR: Who are you?

WALTON: A friend.

VICTOR: Leave me.

WALTON: How can I do that, now?
You would perish.

VICTOR: You have a vessel?

WALTON: For the moment.
Winter coming on, and we are
running out of sea-room.

VICTOR: Where are you bound?

WALTON: Does it matter?
Anywhere would be safer—

VICTOR: *(Insistent)*
But where?

(Pause)

WALTON: The men would like to turn back,
before we're trapped, and the ship is crushed.

VICTOR: And you?

WALTON: I want to go on.
North.
All the way to the Pole,
if there's a way—

VICTOR: Ah yes, well—isn't that the most terrible secret?
There is always a way.
And we find it.
I myself am going North:
to seek the one who fled from me.

(Uneasy, WALTON looks around.)

WALTON: Someone else is here?

(VICTOR nods.)

WALTON: Who is he?

(VICTOR is silent.)

WALTON: What do you want of him?

VICTOR: You told me you were a friend.
If indeed you are, then your life is in danger.

Go, before the doom that shadows me
falls on you, as well.

WALTON: *(Challenged)*
I'm not afraid of dying.

VICTOR: Then maybe I should tell you my story.
Because, I think, I can make you afraid.

WALTON: You can try. But I've been assured—
"no man goes to hell before his time."

VICTOR: My father would have disagreed.
He would have said there was no Hell to go to.
He was mistaken.

(As WALTON listens, VICTOR begins to tell his story.)

Scene Three

(VICTOR's childhood home. VICTOR's FATHER and MOTHER enter, followed by VICTOR's cousin ELIZABETH.)

(FATHER is reading a paper. VICTOR and ELIZABETH are children.)

MOTHER: Victor? Don't make faces at your cousin.
(To ELIZABETH:) And don't you return them.
(To FATHER, too brightly, trying to make conversation)
What is happening? Anywhere in the world.

FATHER: *(Buried in his paper)*
Russia is still at war with Turkey.

MOTHER: Whatever for, I wonder....

FATHER: The King of Sweden has been assassinated.

MOTHER: *(Shaking her head)*
His poor wife...

FATHER: The French peasants are revolting.

MOTHER: Haven't you always felt them to be?

(FATHER gives MOTHER a look. Flustered, she looks around, realizing a child is missing.)

MOTHER: Victor, where is your brother?
(Calling out:)
William?
(Back to VICTOR:)
And must you play with your oatmeal?

VICTOR: *(To FATHER)*
How fast is the guillotine—
when it falls?

MOTHER: What is a "guillotine"?

FATHER: *(Bemused by VICTOR's question)*
How fast?

VICTOR: Does the head have time to think,
"I am being lopped off"?
Is the blade that keen?

FATHER: I don't believe they are killing children—yet.
Though I'm sure they would make an exception,
if you would like to book a passage.

MOTHER: Papa!

VICTOR: If it were so fast that my eyes could still see,
when they held me up by my hair,
would I look down, and would I mutter,
"Don't drop me into that basket
with the other severed heads"?

ELIZABETH: How would you mutter?

VICTOR: What do you mean?

ELIZABETH: Well, your head would be here,
and your lungs would be there.
You wouldn't have the breath to move your lips.

(MOTHER glares at FATHER.)

MOTHER: You *will* insist on reading the morning gazette
at the breakfast table.
The children brood all day,
and then they have horrible dreams at night.

FATHER: *(Winking at the young ones)* So do I.

VICTOR: My porridge is cold.

MOTHER: And lumpy as well, I'd like to hope.
Elizabeth?

(In a huff, MOTHER *exits, followed by the reluctant*
ELIZABETH. FATHER *continues to read the paper.)*

VICTOR: Papa? Is there a God?

FATHER: No. *(He turns a page.)*

VICTOR: Papa? Am *I* a God?

FATHER: If you like.
I felt it was too much bother.
But you could give it a try.

(Folding his paper up, FATHER *exits.)*

Scene Four

(Back in the present, on the iceberg)

WALTON: And did you? Make an attempt?

VICTOR: I succeeded.

WALTON: Not the most impressive of gods.

VICTOR: Christ, you remember, had a few awkward
moments, while he was dangling.

(Suddenly, the offstage DOGS *begin to bark—loudly, frantic.
Anxious,* WALTON *takes a firm grip on his pistol.)*

WALTON: What could have gotten their wind up?

VICTOR: *(Fearing his real guess)* Maybe a walrus—
or a polar bear.

(With the dogs in danger, WALTON *wonders why* VICTOR *isn't moving.)*

WALTON: If you lose your team—

VICTOR: I proceed on foot.

(With VICTOR *being no help,* WALTON *starts to move off, to rescue the dogs.* VICTOR *snaps:)*

VICTOR: Stay where you are!

*(*WALTON *stops, surprised.)*

WALTON: Why?

VICTOR: The dogs are telling me no-one should move.

WALTON: *(Wondering if* VICTOR *is mad)* Are you certain
you heard them correctly?

VICTOR: I used to speak fluent Dog, when I was a child.
And Cat—a little more difficult—
and a smattering of Hill and Tree and Cloud—
and I would lie down in the sun,
in the grass, and be so very still,
I could hear the whole wide world.
Breathing.
In and out—trembling:
alive.
How was that possible?
Alive.
What could that mean?
To be here in the light, in the world
for only a moment,
and gone forever...

WALTON: You've been alone too long, my friend.
Let me see to the dogs...

(WALTON *starts to exit again.* VICTOR *keeps talking, to hold him back.*)

VICTOR: I started on my journey with six.
Four of them died, on the way.
Do you think they went to hell?
Or heaven—either way, some place...

WALTON: Does a dog have a soul?

VICTOR: Do you?

(*From off, we hear a terrible cry of animal pain—and then silence.* WALTON, *spurred to action, runs off. Anxious,* VICTOR *watches him go, talking out loud to keep his fear at bay.*)

VICTOR: I don't.
(*Pause*)
About cats—of course, they made claims:
but who could tell when they were lying?

(*The lights change.*)

Scene Five

(*Two* DOGS *of* VICTOR's *childhood pursue a screeching* CAT *onstage. Chasing them all, but far behind, is* VICTOR's *friend* CLERVAL. DOGS, CAT *and* CLERVAL—*yelping—run in crazy circles around young* VICTOR *[who's almost an adolescent, now.] The menagerie runs off—but* VICTOR *snags* CLERVAL *by the collar, stopping him short.*)

VICTOR: Clerval—do the animals want you to play?

CLERVAL: I don't know.

VICTOR: Did you ask them?

(CLERVAL *considers this, and then dashes off.*)

CLERVAL: Rufus! Annabelle—wait!
I have a question for you!...

(CLERVAL *is gone. A second later, the* CAT—*with* DOGS
in mad pursuit—runs in from another direction. The CAT
leaps into VICTOR'*s arms. Not knowing how their prey has
escaped, the* DOGS *run off.* VICTOR *puts down the smug*
CAT.)

VICTOR: A satisfactory morning, then, Mister Puss—
tormenting the dogs?

CAT: It passed the time.

VICTOR: They are very silly animals.
You ought to be ashamed.

CAT: I'm not.
God gave me a duty. I fulfill it.

VICTOR: Papa says there is no God.
(He takes out a knife)
So it's entirely possible,
that while I perform my experiments—
I am going to be a surgeon, you know—
you may have to suffer unbearably.

CAT: *(Nervous, but hiding it)*
I don't follow....

VICTOR: No-one to stop me.

CAT: Ah.
(Pause)
There is a god of cats.
He's very large.
Unpleasantly large.
Big.
Some of us believe he coughed up this.
(It gestures around him.)

VICTOR: The earth is a fur-ball?
That's absurd.

CAT: And a talking cat would be....

VICTOR: Very clever.

CAT: But not quite clever enough
to escape your shiny knife.

(Pause)

VICTOR: The century is turning—
men are doing incredible things.
When they pass an electric current
through a dead frog's leg—
can you guess what happens?

CAT: People stare at them, wondering why they would
want to pass an electric current through a dead frog's
leg?

VICTOR: The leg comes back to life!
It twitches. Dangling on a spike,
attached to nothing, it suddenly—moves!

CAT: *(Thinking fast)*
I already have an electrical current. Inside me.

VICTOR: *(Agreeing, excited)*
Do you think so?

CAT: Look!
(He demonstrates an impressive array of twitches.)
Out of nowhere. "Ex nihilo!"
I don't need to be impaled.

VICTOR: But why do we die?
The current stops.
Why does the spark go out?

CAT: It's a mystery.

VICTOR: That's why I have to cut you open.

(At that moment ELIZABETH *enters.)*

ELIZABETH: *(Gently chiding)*
Cousin? What are you doing?

VICTOR: Explaining fate to the cat.

ELIZABETH: *(To rescue the animal)*
Shoo!

(The CAT, *irate at having been frightened, runs off.*
VICTOR *regards* ELIZABETH.*)*

ELIZABETH: Where is your friend Clerval?

VICTOR: You like him.

ELIZABETH: Oh yes: we are going to run away.

VICTOR: He told me he thought you were beautiful.

ELIZABETH: Did he? While he was trotting beside you,
hoping you would scruff his fur?

VICTOR: Will you marry me?

ELIZABETH: I don't think so. No.

VICTOR: Why not?

ELIZABETH: Because you expect me to.

VICTOR: But you love me.

ELIZABETH: I don't care. I will not be a part of your
collection.
I'm not the tusk of a narwhal.
Or an albino alligator.
Or something that ought to be free,
pinned to a board, for you to study.

*(*VICTOR *points at a dull red stain on her dress.)*

VICTOR: Did you hurt yourself?

ELIZABETH: *(Looking down, startled)*
No!

VICTOR: You're bleeding.

ELIZABETH: Am I?

*(*ELIZABETH, *dreading her own understanding, tries to fight
down her panic.)*

Your mother said I would.
I thought she was only trying to frighten me.
"Regular as the moon—"
so the moon isn't beautiful, not any more.
I can have a baby, now,
and suffer, having it, and die.

(VICTOR *doesn't know what to say.*)

ELIZABETH: Like my mama did, giving birth to me.
Blood is running down my leg.
Do something.
Please.
I'm afraid.

(VICTOR *kneels at her feet. Lifting up the edge of her skirt,
he touches her blood with his fingertips.*)

ELIZABETH: I smell like a butcher's shop.

VICTOR: No, not at all: you smell alive.

(*He buries his face in her skirt. Touched by his lack of
revulsion, she strokes his head.*)

ELIZABETH: I tore my mother open.
I'm afraid.

VICTOR: Then don't ever marry.

ELIZABETH: I may have to.

VICTOR: Why? Tell me.

ELIZABETH: Because I have always loved you.
I have always wanted to touch your hair...
twist it around my fingers,
pull it tight, till you cried out
and I'd silence you with my kisses.

VICTOR: That would be—love?

ELIZABETH: (*Annoyed*)
I don't think you could ever feel that way.

You love me because I'm an animal.
You love me because I bleed.

(Upset—at what, she can't be sure—she pushes him away from her.)

VICTOR: I don't understand you!

ELIZABETH: I *know*! Why do you think I've always hated you?

(ELIZABETH rushes off. Bewildered, VICTOR watches her go. Then he looks at the blood on his hands. The serving-girl JUSTINE passes by.)

VICTOR: Justine—would you bring me a cloth?

JUSTINE: Yes sir.

VICTOR: *(Feeling he needs to explain)*
I cut myself.

JUSTINE: You ought to be careful.
(She starts to exit.)

VICTOR: Justine—if you were bleeding,
and I asked you why—
would you hate me?

JUSTINE: If I was bleeding, sir?
Where?

VICTOR: It doesn't matter where!
But if I were concerned—

JUSTINE: About me?

VICTOR: Well, curious, then.

JUSTINE: I could never hate you, sir.

VICTOR: Why not?

JUSTINE: Why not? I would lose my job.

(As JUSTINE moves off, lights change.)

Scene Six

(Back on the iceberg. An offstage gunshot jerks VICTOR *back to the present.* WALTON *re-enters, a smear of blood on his coat.)*

WALTON: *(Explaining the gunshot)*
Something was moving, I thought, in the shadows...
I was startled: I fired.
(Trying to reassure himself)
Only a trick of the light.

VICTOR: But you're hurt.

WALTON: No.

VICTOR: You're bleeding.

WALTON: Am I?
(He looks at his coat.)
It isn't my blood.
I found one of the dogs.
What was left of it—
it had been torn apart.
Its guts were spilling out on the ice.

(Judging VICTOR's *reaction)*

WALTON: And you aren't surprised.
Who are you?

VICTOR: My name is Victor Frankenstein.

WALTON: That means nothing to me.
Who *are* you?

VICTOR: What am I being accused of, Mister...?

WALTON: "Captain." Robert Walton.

VICTOR: Putting your life in jeopardy?
I warned you: RUN AWAY!

WALTON: Do you think I give a god damn, sir,
if you're reckless of my safety?
Look what I have done:
I've led a shipful of men to their doom.

VICTOR: And you seem to be proud of that.

WALTON: Not proud...

VICTOR: Then what—ashamed?
I hope you aren't seeking absolution.

(WALTON *stands up to Victor's challenge.*)

WALTON: When I saw you, on the ice, I thought
I might have found the one man
who could understand why I had to come here.

VICTOR: Into this—nothing...

WALTON: Or into what lies beyond it.
Don't you wonder?

(VICTOR *decides to acknowledge their connection.*)

VICTOR: What does it say in the Bible?
"A valley full of bones..."

WALTON: *(Recognizing the quote)*
"...and behold they were very many, and dry—
and can these bones live?"

VICTOR: Can they?
I did wonder.
So I began to investigate.

(*Lights change.*)

Scene Seven

(VICTOR is rubbing a rod made of glass, with a piece of fur, when his younger brother WILLIAM dashes on stage, yelling at the top of his lungs.)

WILLIAM: Victor! Victor! Victor! Victor! Victor! Victor! Victor! Victor!

(Distracted by the experiment he's conducting, VICTOR doesn't even look up, until WILLIAM's already dashing off.)

VICTOR: What?

(But WILLIAM is gone, as VICTOR's MOTHER enters.)

MOTHER: Victor, where is the cat?

VICTOR: I haven't seen it.

MOTHER: Why don't I believe you?

VICTOR: Because your life has been a succession of nagging disappointments?

(Pause)

MOTHER: *(Pointing to VICTOR's materials)* Explain that bedraggled pelt in your hand.

VICTOR: It's for an experiment—
I use it to rub a glass rod, like so—
and the rod becomes electrical—

MOTHER: But *what is it*?

VICTOR: It's a scrap of fur. I found it in the woods.

(Pause)

MOTHER: Do you know the words of the oath you will have to swear, when you become a physician?

VICTOR: "First, do no harm."

MOTHER: I was fond of that cat.

VICTOR: The cat was subject to fits.

MOTHER: And who among us is not?
Your brother runs around the house,
screaming "Victor! Victor! Victor!"

(Pause)

VICTOR: If I touch you with this rod,
every hair on your head will stand on end.

MOTHER: Or, to achieve the same effect,
I can contemplate my life—
a few minutes from now,
when you and your brother are grown,
your cousin is married,
your father is dead,
for no reason but spite—
and I'm alone.

(MOTHER *takes the piece of fur from* VICTOR, *looking at it
with regret, as she exits.* WILLIAM *comes galloping back
onstage, still yelling.*)

WILLIAM: Victor! Victor! Victor! Victor!
Victor! Victor! Victor!

VICTOR: *What?*

WILLIAM: If you say a word over and over and over,
it doesn't mean anything any more.
It's just a sound. Have you noticed that?
(Demonstrating)
"The." "The." "The." "The." "The."—
what does "the" mean?

VICTOR: I don't know.

WILLIAM: Then why do we say it?

VICTOR: Why do we say anything?

WILLIAM: Because, if it's too quiet...

VICTOR: *(Intrigued)*
Go on...

WILLIAM: It's too quiet! Victor! Victor! Victor!

(Gleefully shouting his brother's name, WILLIAM runs off, as VICTOR's FATHER enters, a shovel in his hand.)

FATHER: Could I ask if you deliberately
set out to provoke your mother?

VICTOR: Papa, we were simply talking—

FATHER: Nothing is simple, with that woman.
Now she's dragging me off to the churchyard.

VICTOR: Why?

FATHER: Exactly! It's not even Sunday.
(He pulls out the piece of fur.)
But we have to bury this.

VICTOR: For what reason?

FATHER: Your mother says it's the cat:
the one who—wisely, in my opinion—
decamped, some time ago.

(FATHER waits for VICTOR to dispute this.)

VICTOR: It's just a piece of fur.

FATHER: Then what a waste of an afternoon:
to be in that godforsaken churchyard,
digging a hole for a—pelt,
while your mother wanders off, to visit the
graves of your brothers and sisters.

VICTOR: I am sorry, Papa.

FATHER: For what? A mistake I made, long ago,
in my reckless youth?
(He starts to exit.)
Don't ever marry.

VICTOR: Not even for love?

FATHER: Do you think I hunted your mother down for her money?

(When VICTOR's FATHER *is gone,* VICTOR *remembers* WILLIAM's *"experiment" .)*

VICTOR: "Dead, dead, dead, dead...
DEAD. DEAD. DEAD..."

(Hearing VICTOR *playing his "game",* WILLIAM *runs back in to play with him.)*

VICTOR & WILLIAM: *(Together)*
"DEAD! DEAD! DEAD! DEAD!
DEAD! DEAD! DEAD!"

WILLIAM: See? It's not a word anymore.
It's just a great thud.
(He runs off, continuing his chant of "Dead, dead...")

VICTOR: *(Shaking his head)*
If only it were.
(Coming to a new resolution:)
I need to learn so much more...

(The lights change.)

Scene Eight

(The parlor. VICTOR's FATHER *has just received a letter. He calls out.)*

FATHER: News from the university...

*(*VICTOR's MOTHER *and* ELIZABETH *come hurrying in.)*

MOTHER: Victor has deigned to honor us
with another letter? What a treat!
That would make—how many—
a total of three—in as many years?

*(*FATHER *ignores her, reading the letter.)*

FATHER: He's disenchanted, he says,
with the physical sciences.

MOTHER: So am I—I think.

FATHER: Something about a "world elsewhere".
(Surprised)
He's reading Paracelsus.

MOTHER: Who?

FATHER: A great charlatan of the Middle Ages
modern science left behind.
An alchemist—

MOTHER: *Alchemy?* Won't Victor go directly to hell?

FATHER: *(Reading on:)*
In fact, where he seems to be bound is home.

ELIZABETH: *(Thrilled)*
Victor is coming back to us?

(MOTHER *grabs the letter.)*

MOTHER: What? And you didn't tell me?

FATHER: He only brings it up in the postscript.

MOTHER: *(Reading, appalled)*
He is being—sent down?

FATHER: Apparently there was an accident—

MOTHER: *(Reading)*
He blew up the chemistry hall?

FATHER: But he's not discouraged, he says.
He'll continue his research—in our cellar.

Scene Nine

(Another part of the house. As VICTOR *crosses, lost in a book he's reading,* CLERVAL *enters, holding something wrapped in a handkerchief. Blood is starting to seep through the cloth.)*

CLERVAL: Victor?

VICTOR: What are you doing with that?

CLERVAL: You know what it is?

VICTOR: It's a specimen.

CLERVAL: Could you enlighten me as to the species?
I only ask, because—

VICTOR: Clerval—

CLERVAL: Yes I know, there are mysteries you are intent
on solving—
the "What is life?" sort of thing,
and ordinarily I would never presume to inquire
into your methods—

VICTOR: I seem to remember telling you never to
go in the cellar, Clerval.

CLERVAL: You gave me a key.

VICTOR: In case I went down there to work
and never came back up.
But here I am—I have not gone missing.
And yet you decided the time had come
to intrude upon my privacy.

*(*CLERVAL *holds up the bloody packet.)*

CLERVAL: Victor, this is still warm.

VICTOR: Is it? And how could you have known that
before you went down the cellar stairs?

(Pause)

CLERVAL: I had a dream about you, last night.
We were on a walking-tour,
up into some highlands I'd never seen before,
deep summer, blazing hot, and when we
came to a tarn, you wanted to bathe.
But I held back—there was something
about the water: how very still it was,
and how dark—and you were laughing at me:
"What are you afraid of?"
And then you took a step closer to me
and you kissed me on the mouth.

(Pause)

(VICTOR *approaches his friend. Very deliberately,*
he kisses him. CLERVAL *is stunned.)*

VICTOR: Don't waste a good dream on
something you can have.
Dream about the impossible.

(VICTOR *takes the cloth-wrapped thing from* CLERVAL.)

VICTOR: This is warm because I passed an electrical
current through it.

CLERVAL: Why?

VICTOR: Why did you want me to kiss you?

CLERVAL: I didn't!

VICTOR: Because you were curious.

(Pause)

CLERVAL: If I were the curious sort,
I might have looked under that bloody tarpaulin
you had thrown over something—god knows what—
in the darkest part of the cellar.

VICTOR: *(Suddenly very anxious)*
Did you?

CLERVAL: No.

VICTOR: Why not?

CLERVAL: Because I was afraid.
The tarpaulin moved.

(For a moment, VICTOR is taken aback.)

CLERVAL: Then a rat scurried out from under the cloth.
There was a slick of blood, on its muzzle.
Victor, what was it feeding on?

VICTOR: Any number of my hopes.

Scene Ten

(In a cellar room that VICTOR uses for his experiments.
VICTOR enters, approaching a blood-stained tarpaulin.
He pulls the tarpaulin off. A naked CREATURE slumps in a
straight-backed chair. It appears to be dead. Stitched together
from severed body parts, it looks like the mangled corpse of a
man who was in a terrible accident. VICTOR sits in a chair,
beside the CREATURE. He stares at his creation.)

VICTOR: Who made you?
I made you.
Bones I stole from the slaughter-house
and muscle from a dissecting room,
skin I would peel, one bloody sheet at a time,
from my own body,
the brain of a child who was trampled to death
right in front of me, by a runaway carriage—
why did no-one ever miss that child,
when I gathered up the remains?
Why did no-one claim the cadavers
growing mould in the anatomy halls,
the ones I would whittle away at,
late at night, a lip, an eye,
a finger tucked away in my pocket—
why did it matter to no-one, anywhere,

that these bodies had been alive?
(Pause)
Did no-one lie awake at night,
missing the touch of that hand,
or the weight of those legs, across their own,
or the muscles moving under the skin
of the back, the back arching up:
this man looking down on his love, with delight—
Does no-one stare up at the dark
and try to remember what you looked like?

(In frustration, VICTOR *hauls the inanimate* CREATURE *to its feet. He struggles to hold it upright, willing it to stand.)*

VICTOR: "I look like death."
The spark goes out.
Why does the spark go out?
And why can I never bring it back?

(The CREATURE's *silence is terrible.)*

VICTOR: WHY DOESN'T ANYONE REMEMBER
ANY PART OF YOU?
A lock of hair, a breath, a single smile...
Like you never existed.

(The dead weight is too much. VICTOR *roughly drops the* CREATURE *back in the chair—but the chair tips over, and the* CREATURE *sprawls on the floor, in a grotesque heap.)*

VICTOR: You *didn't* exist.
I made you.
But I cannot make the spark.

*(*ELIZABETH *appears at the door to the cellar.)*

ELIZABETH: Victor? Are you all right?
Did you fall?

VICTOR: What are you doing, Elizabeth?

ELIZABETH: I am standing here, with my hand on the door,

remembering your clear instruction
never to try the lock.
(Pause)
But I heard you stumble.

VICTOR: I ran into something.
The cellar is dark, and
my candle is nearly out.

ELIZABETH: Shall I bring you another?

(Pause)

VICTOR: No.
My experiment failed. Again.
I am gnashing my teeth.

(Pause)

ELIZABETH: My hand is still on the door.
Will you let me in?

(We hear a distant rumble.)

VICTOR: What was that? Was that thunder?

(Looking at the fallen CREATURE, VICTOR *has an idea.)*

Scene Eleven

(A flash of lightning. WILLIAM *runs on, holding the string
of a kite that is flying high up, offstage. There's an ominous
rumble of thunder.)*

VICTOR: *(Offstage)*
Willie! Bring it back!

WILLIAM: *(Exhilarated)*
I can't! The kite is pulling me into the air!

MOTHER: *(Offstage)*
William Frankenstein!

WILLIAM: I can't come down! I'm flying! Look!

(MOTHER *hurries on.*)

MOTHER: Give the string to your brother! *Victor?*

(*Another flash of lightning*)

WILLIAM: Hurrah! The storm is on top of us!
That one almost hit!
Victor, hurry!

(VICTOR *enters, holding an early version of a battery,
a Leyden jar. Thunder rumbles.* ELIZABETH *and* VICTOR's
friend CLERVAL *comes in.*)

VICTOR: Willie, the kite is dangerous now.

CLERVAL: (*Making trouble, to* VICTOR)
But why can *your* eyeballs explode? And no-one else's?
I want a turn.

WILLIAM: My eyes will explode?

MOTHER: Thank you so much for you help, Clerval.
(*To* WILLIAM)
Give your brother the kite-string—now!

WILLIAM: No!

VICTOR: It's all right: the part he's holding is silk.
It doesn't conduct—I think....

MOTHER: You *think?*
(*To anyone*)
And what do you mean by "conduct"?

CLERVAL: (*Aware of* WILLIAM's *game*)
Nothing! "Conduct, conduct, conduct, conduct—"

(*A flash of lightning, a terrible clap of thunder*)

MOTHER: I HAVE BURIED SEVEN CHILDREN!
NONE OF THIS IS REMOTELY AMUSING!

(*Her anger sobers everyone.*)

MOTHER: Now give your brother the kite,
you little monster. Do you hear me?
(Pointing off)
Or would you like to be reduced to that?
A rotting stump?

(WILLIAM's on the verge of tears, as MOTHER storms off.)

WILLIAM: Why is she cross at me?

CLERVAL: She isn't, Willie. She's only remembering:
that stump was once a beautiful oak
we used to climb to the very top—

WILLIAM: What happened to it?

CLERVAL: A storm came up, as sudden as this one.
We'd barely time to get to the house.
And just as we'd tumbled inside, sopping,
there was a scalding light,
and a roar that rattled all the window-panes,
and when we looked back at the tree,
the tree was gone.

WILLIAM: Gone where?

CLERVAL: Exploded.
Scraps of bark and leaf,
and a blackened stump. Nothing else.

(WILLIAM, shaken, hands the string of the kite to VICTOR.)

WILLIAM: I found the bones of a robin, once,
and a worm crawled out of the eye-hole.

CLERVAL: The worm was eating the bird?

WILLIAM: It isn't funny!
(To VICTOR)
What will be left of *you*?
(He runs off.)

ELIZABETH: *(Reproving)*
A bone. A brittle bit of skin. A tooth—

VICTOR: Would you not be womanish now?
Be useful. Here—hold the Leyden jar,
while I attach the string, like so—

*(He attaches the kite-string—above the silk thread he was
using to insulate himself—to a metal rod that sticks out of the
lid of the apparatus* ELIZABETH *is holding. Nervous about
this experiment,* CLERVAL *begins to ramble.)*

CLERVAL: I haven't thought of that tree in years.
Remember how it would sway in the wind,
when we stood in the top-most boughs?
It was like sailing. Too much like—
being tossed about in the crow's-nest:
Lizzie, have you forgotten the time
you were sea-sick?
Or was that me—

*(Suddenly, a blare of light—and directly above them,
a shattering clap of thunder. For a moment, everyone
is stunned. Then* VICTOR *realizes the jar is glowing.)*

VICTOR: Elizabeth—put down the jar. PUT IT DOWN.

(She doesn't move.)

ELIZABETH: Am I dead?
Is hell Clerval, chattering on and on forever?
(To VICTOR*)*
Did I never get to lie beneath you,
in the high grass, in the heat of the day,
and feel the slick of your skin,
and taste your mouth, and hear you whisper
hot in my ear, "Don't move!—
stay still, so very still, if you buck
and I slip any deeper inside you
I am gone" —and I want that,
both of us, into each other,
exploding, so I *do* buck—
and we both cry out,

on the edge, falling into ourselves
and a light streams out of us...

(Carefully VICTOR *takes the jar from* ELIZABETH.
She starts to come out of her trance.)

ELIZABETH: Why are you looking at me like that?
I was babbling. What did I say?

VICTOR: *(Very gently)*
Only—that you were afraid of dying.

(He detaches the string of the kite, absently handing it to
CLERVAL.)

CLERVAL: What happens now?

VICTOR: *(With renewed purpose)*
I set us all free.
I make a dead frog-leg dance.

*(*VICTOR *exits, with the glowing jar.* ELIZABETH *and*
CLERVAL, *both rattled, watch him go. Finally,* CLERVAL
shouts out:)

CLERVAL: COME BACK!
MAKE ELIZABETH DANCE!

*(*ELIZABETH *stares at* CLERVAL. *Then she slaps him.)*

ELIZABETH: He doesn't love either one of us.
Could you try not to be so pathetic?

*(*CLERVAL *is speechless. Regretful,* ELIZABETH *touches his
face.)*

ELIZABETH: Did I hurt you?

CLERVAL: Yes.

ELIZABETH: I'm sorry.
Or I would certainly like to be.

*(They regard each other. Barely aware of what they do,
they move into each other's arms. They kiss—gently at first,
and then with a growing, desperate passion. Another flash*

of lightning—not as near—and a growl of thunder.
Coming out of their trance, CLERVAL *and* ELIZABETH
step away from each other. Confused and upset, ELIZABETH
*runs off. Watching her go—and dazed himself—*CLERVAL
releases the kite. It floats off into the sky.)

Scene Twelve

(The cellar-room. The lifeless naked CREATURE *again is*
slumped in a chair. VICTOR *enters, in his hands the glowing*
Leyden jar. On the brink of success, he hesitates—fearful of
failure. He stares at the CREATURE.*)*

VICTOR: You don't know this, but a general rain
is falling over the countryside.
People are trapped in their rooms,
by a dying fire—if they can afford even that—
watching the flames sink down,
trying not to think of how very little
will ever become of their lives:
they have hopes, but they come to nothing,
they have dreams that die, unborn,
and the ones who love them wait in vain
to be given anything in return...

(The CREATURE *is silent.)*

VICTOR: I have nothing to give—
I have emptied myself into you:
my dream, my hope. And if I fail—
if I turn back now...

(With a sudden and savage motion, VICTOR *touches the*
metal rod of the Leyden jar to the CREATURE's *chest. The*
CREATURE *jerks. It opens its eyes. It screams. The scream is*
uncanny, terrifying. VICTOR *takes a step backward, staring*
at what he has wrought. The scream stops, just as suddenly
as it started. The CREATURE *slumps in the chair again, inert.)*

VICTOR: Dead again. Or were you ever alive?
Were you only a frog-leg twitching?
(Pause)
I have brought you to a door.
Why won't you go through it?
GO THROUGH THE DOOR!

*(Deciding to put his life on the line, VICTOR very deliberately
drops his hand on top of the Leyden jar. As the current runs
through him, he touches the CREATURE, who screams—
as VICTOR shouts over him.)*

VICTOR: The angel of "Revelations"—
what does he promise: "There shall be time no longer!"
And time is nothing else but death—so
why do we have to wait for the sound of trumpets
at the Apocalypse?
I declare that from this moment, there will be death
no longer—
And a stream of light, a torrent
will come roaring, headlong, into our dark world.

*(At the end of his adrenaline-rush, VICTOR falls backward,
lying where he fell. The Leyden jar rolls across the floor
and comes to rest. The CREATURE stands unsteadily.
He approaches VICTOR. Getting down on all fours,
he crawls atop his creator. He touches VICTOR's face,
his neck—becoming aware of the pulse at Victor's throat.)*

CREATURE: *(Softly)*
Boom, boom, boom, boom, boom, boom, boom—

*(Coming to, with a jolt, VICTOR grabs the CREATURE's hand
and forces it off him. VICTOR stares at his creation, horrified
and amazed.)*

CREATURE: I want....

VICTOR: What?

*(The CREATURE shakes his head, unable to be any more
articulate.)*

CREATURE: I WANT.

(JUSTINE, *the serving-girl, appears at the cellar door.*)

JUSTINE: Mister Frankenstein?

(*The* CREATURE *turns his head, at the sound of a woman's voice.*)

JUSTINE: (*Off*) I heard you cry out.
Are you all right?

(*The* CREATURE *is frightened by this new voice.*
VICTOR *uses his fear.*)

VICTOR: (*To the* CREATURE)
Hide! If anyone finds you,
they will hurt you. Do you understand?

CREATURE: Pain...

VICTOR: Yes!

JUSTINE: (*Off*)
You left the door ajar.
You must have been in a terrible hurry.

VICTOR: (*To the* CREATURE, *pointing off*)
There, in the shadows. Go!

(*But the* CREATURE, *though afraid, is confused.* VICTOR *has to guide him—forcefully—into a hiding-place [behind the chair, or a table], as* JUSTINE *speaks.*)

JUSTINE: (*Off*)
Did you fall down the stairs?
Would you mind if I had a look at you, in a puddle of blood?

(VICTOR *covers the hiding* CREATURE *with the tarp— just as* JUSTINE *warily enters this forbidden place.*)

VICTOR: Justine, I wasn't hurt.
So go away—now.
You're in terrible danger...

JUSTINE: Of course I am. Not that I
mistake myself for a beauty,
it's only—"Here I am. You can have me."
Grab a tit, and *I* can scream—
will anyone come to my rescue?

(Now ELIZABETH *appears at the top of the cellar stairs.)*

ELIZABETH: Victor? No-one can find Justine.
Have you seen her?

VICTOR: No!
I will be right up.

(As VICTOR *speaks, the* CREATURE *starts to come out of his
hiding-place—approaching* JUSTINE, *who doesn't see him
yet.)*

JUSTINE: When you tell a lie, like that,
do you think it leaves a stink in the air?

VICTOR: What you smell are some of my chemicals—
in retorts I forget about, until they're
boiling over.

*(*VICTOR *tries—without alerting* JUSTINE*—to step between
her and the* CREATURE, *who's very close now.)*

JUSTINE: Worse than that. Like a fat old rat
had died in the walls—it's sickening.

(Before VICTOR *can stop him, the* CREATURE *puts a hand on*
JUSTINE'*s neck. She gasps, thinking it's* VICTOR.*)*

VICTOR: Cold?

JUSTINE: *(Not looking around)*
As the grave.
What is wrong with you?

VICTOR: I'm dying. And so are the people I love—
even you, who I hardly know at all—
and every other living soul,

we are racing to oblivion.
And I have been trying to remedy that—

JUSTINE: *(Dumbfounded)*
—by finding a cure—for death.

VICTOR: Yes.

(The tension finally overcomes JUSTINE, who starts to laugh.)

JUSTINE: I myself was of a mind that death
was a cure for life.

*(The CREATURE suddenly silences her, by putting his other
hand on her neck.)*

CREATURE: Boom, boom, boom, boom...

*(VICTOR unthinkingly takes a step away from JUSTINE.
She realizes he isn't standing behind her.)*

JUSTINE: Begging your pardon, sir,
but you seem to be—there,
and your hands are here—

VICTOR: *(To the CREATURE)*
Let go of her.
Let go.

(Reluctantly, the CREATURE takes his hands away.)

CREATURE: I want....

*(Fearful, JUSTINE turns and sees the CREATURE, for the first
time. They stare at each other.)*

VICTOR: Justine? This is only a dream.

JUSTINE: No.

VICTOR: All right—but can you pretend it is?

JUSTINE: Where did it come from?

VICTOR: Here and there.

JUSTINE: Where will it live?
It *is* alive?

CREATURE: I want to go—home.

JUSTINE: Back to the grave.

CREATURE: *(Contradicting)*
Home.

VICTOR: *(The scientist, amazed)*
There are memories still left
in the brain I gave him—
how is that possible?
(To the CREATURE*)*
Where is home?

CREATURE: A fire. Voices...

VICTOR: What are they saying?

(Pause)

CREATURE: "Who made you?"

*(*JUSTINE *points at* VICTOR*.)*

JUSTINE: He made you.

(Pause)

CREATURE: Pain. Up and down me. All over me.
Why do I hurt?

JUSTINE: Because he made you.

(Pause)

CREATURE: Help me.

JUSTINE: If I could, I would.
I would kill you.

CREATURE: HELP ME!

JUSTINE: *No.* No—

(Suddenly JUSTINE *runs away.* VICTOR *starts after her.)*

VICTOR: Justine!

(But the CREATURE *stops him.)*

CREATURE: I want to go home.

VICTOR: I don't know where that is.

CREATURE: A fire. Voices.

(As VICTOR *replies, the* CREATURE *moves away.)*

VICTOR: Once upon a time.
Those things are gone, now.

*(*ELIZABETH *appears at the top of the cellar stairs.)*

ELIZABETH: Victor?

(He doesn't answer. The CREATURE *looks up at this new
voice.)*

ELIZABETH: Something has happened.
Justine is having a kind of—fit,
she's sobbing on the kitchen floor,
and she won't let anyone near her.

(Pause. The CREATURE *remembers* JUSTINE.*)*

CREATURE: I said, "Help me"
But she didn't. "Justine."
If she could, she would kill me.

VICTOR: You have it all in a jumble—

ELIZABETH: Victor?

(Pause)

VICTOR: Yes!

ELIZABETH: I am coming down.
Is that all right?

*(*VICTOR *doesn't answer.* ELIZABETH *hesitates, then starts to
descend.* VICTOR *turns to the* CREATURE, *seeking a better
hiding place.)*

VICTOR: Back into the dark.

CREATURE: I hurt!

(VICTOR herds the CREATURE into the darkest part of the cellar.)

VICTOR: I understand—

CREATURE: Every part of me.

VICTOR: Can you be very quiet?

CREATURE: Why did you wake me?

VICTOR: I made a mistake.

CREATURE: I *hurt*!

VICTOR: I will help you!—
but only be still.

(The CREATURE does as he's told. VICTOR steps back into the light as ELIZABETH appears, looking about at this place she's seldom seen.)

ELIZABETH: You don't mind that the walls are wet....

VICTOR: Not at all. I find the chill keeps me awake.

ELIZABETH: Ah. You could work in a room with windows.

VICTOR: I could watch the shadows of clouds moving over the lawn, and get nothing done.

ELIZABETH: What is that smell?

VICTOR: Another in a series of failed experiments.

(Pause)

ELIZABETH: Do you remember, when we were younger, I was afraid of having children?
I'm not, anymore. I'm not.
You don't have to interfere with the servants.

VICTOR: You think very little of me.

ELIZABETH: I think—there is little of you I know.

(Pause)

VICTOR: Do you believe in God?

ELIZABETH: I'm not certain.

VICTOR: Do you believe *I'm* God?

ELIZABETH: Well—you do hide yourself away from the
people who love you.
No-one can find you.
Maybe you *are* God.
Show me your work.

VICTOR: It isn't finished.

(Angry, ELIZABETH turns to leave—but VICTOR stops her.)

VICTOR:—and it would upset you to see it now:
when we were children, remember,
I had a specimen I kept covered?
But you had to pull the cover away,
and what was staring back at you?
The foetus of a pig,
in a jar of alcohol—decomposing.
Not a creature out of a nightmare—
only a humble part of nature.
But disturbing—because it was incomplete—
you screamed.

ELIZABETH: I thought it was moving.

VICTOR: You bumped it—it was sloshing about—

ELIZABETH: I told you: I am older, now.
And my childish fears I've put aside.
If there is a "humble piece of nature"
floating in this dark, let me see it.

VICTOR: No—not now. But soon...
And then there will be no secrets between us.

ELIZABETH: When?

VICTOR: When we are man and wife, at last.
Elizabeth, will you marry me?

(Pause)

ELIZABETH: If you will tell me what you've done.
What has happened in this room?

*(*VICTOR *cannot answer.)*

ELIZABETH: You didn't lie to me. Thank you.
But Victor, my answer is "no".

(At a stalemate, ELIZABETH *hurries out. A moment later,
the* CREATURE *steps out of the shadows.* VICTOR *stares at
him, overwhelmed.)*

CREATURE: Help me.

VICTOR: How?

CREATURE: I want to go home.
A fire. Voices...
(Reaching up, as if to touch something)
Close to the—

VICTOR: What?

CREATURE: *(Remembering the word)*
The—sky.

VICTOR: Maybe you lived in the mountains.
Is that what you mean?

CREATURE: I don't know.

VICTOR: *(Forming a plan)*

High up on a hillside...
I could take you back—would you like that?
Under so many thousand stars,
you can never count them all.

CREATURE: Stars...

VICTOR: Let me show you.

(The lights change.)

Scene Thirteen

(The CREATURE—*wearing ill-fitting clothes of* VICTOR's—
is following his creator up a winding mountain path. Dusk.
VICTOR *lights the way with a flickering lantern.)*

CREATURE: Cold.

VICTOR: You can build a fire.

(The CREATURE *looks about, uncertain.)*

CREATURE: Food.

VICTOR: There is plenty of game about.

CREATURE: *(More insistent)*
Food.

VICTOR: Whatever you catch, you can eat.

CREATURE: Rain...

VICTOR: Stay under the shelter of the trees.

CREATURE: Rain. And then I get wet.

VICTOR: The fire will dry you out.

CREATURE: Beating: "Boom, boom, boom"—
Her arms around me.

(VICTOR is startled.)

CREATURE: Somebody held me.

(Pause)

VICTOR: Your mother. Or a nurse.
That was very long ago.

CREATURE: *(Agitated)*
I WANT—...

(VICTOR, reluctant, takes the CREATURE *in his arms.*
The CREATURE *quiets.)*

CREATURE: When I close my eyes...

VICTOR: *(Giving the name)*
" Dark"

CREATURE: When I open them?

VICTOR: "Light."

CREATURE: But my eyes are open now.
Why is it dark?

VICTOR: Because it's night.

CREATURE: "Night."
Forever and ever.

VICTOR: Just a few hours.
And then the sun will come up again,
it'll be light, and the air will be warmer—
do you remember the word for that? "Day."

CREATURE: It was night.
Forever and ever.

(VICTOR suddenly thinks he knows what the CREATURE is talking about.)

VICTOR: When you were dead? Is that what you mean?
Then it's true—there is nothing after?
I had hoped you could bring me news of another world.
But there is no other.

(The CREATURE doesn't answer. It's staring into VICTOR's eyes, alarmed.)

CREATURE: There is someone in your eyes.

VICTOR: *(Not understanding)*
No.

CREATURE: A tiny man, looking out at me.
A demon. With a shining face.

VICTOR: It's you. It's your reflection.

(The CREATURE *is horrified.)*

CREATURE: Darker! DARKER!

VICTOR: Remember? Close your eyes.

(The CREATURE *does so.)*

CREATURE: Night...

VICTOR: All the long months I was making you—
stitching an arm to a shoulder, hand to a wrist,
threading the nerves, how many thousand,
stretching skin across bone—
I would look at you, splayed across a table
and think you were very beautiful.
Was I wrong? Were you always
as you are now?
Or is it the pain I delivered you into
that made you so very terrible?
(He stares at his creation, knowing what he has to do.)
You were angry at me for waking you.
(Pause)
Go back to sleep.

(While the CREATURE's *eyes are shut,* VICTOR *quietly steals away.)*

CREATURE: Colder.
Night. Forever.
(Remembering:)
But I can open my eyes...

(He does so—and sees that VICTOR *is gone.)*

CREATURE: Victor?
Where are you?
(He looks all around him, panicking.)
WHERE ARE YOU?
VICTOR!

Scene Fourteen

(On the iceberg. WALTON *watches* VICTOR, *uneasy.)*

WALTON: You heard it cry out?

VICTOR: Yes. And I hear it still: "Victor! Victor!"
If I had turned back—
but I left it there.
And then I made my way home.

*(*WALTON *is chilled, realizing what* VICTOR *did.)*

VICTOR: Who have you left behind?
Your mother and father—where are they?
Your wife?

WALTON: I never married.

VICTOR: A sweetheart.

WALTON: No-one.

VICTOR: Why?

WALTON: *(Evading)*
It didn't die—did it?
The creature you dreamed about, and abandoned.

VICTOR: No: it's a very disturbing thing about dreams—
they want to live.

(Pause. The groan and creak of ice are loud.)

WALTON: The ice is starting to break apart.

VICTOR: Go.

WALTON: If you will come with me.

VICTOR: *(Shaking his head)*
I have to stay behind.
I have a rendezvous, in this place.

(Nervously, WALTON *looks out at the dark.)*

WALTON: How did it find you again—
after you left it on the hillside?

VICTOR: I don't know. A year had passed.
I thought I was safe—
What does that mean? "Safe..."
And then, one summer afternoon...
(*He stops, overwhelmed.*)

WALTON: What?

VICTOR: ...at the edge of a meadow...

WALTON: Tell me.

(VICTOR *stares at* WALTON. *The scene changes.*)

Scene Fifteen

(*An empty meadow*)

WILLIAM: (*Off*) Where are you?
(*He runs on, out of breath, and looks around.*)
Where *are* you?

JUSTINE: (*Off*) Here—you little goose.
(*She enters, lugging a heavy picnic-basket.*)

WILLIAM: Why can't you go faster?

JUSTINE: Because I'm old.

WILLIAM: You are. And you never married.
You're an old maid!

JUSTINE: That's right.

WILLIAM: I'll marry you. If you like.

JUSTINE: I wouldn't have you.

WILLIAM: Why not?

JUSTINE: Because you made me carry this basket.

WILLIAM: Isn't that why we have servants?

(JUSTINE *plunks down the basket, hard—we hear the clatter of breaking china.*)

JUSTINE: *(Almost admiring)*
What a horrid little creature you are.

WILLIAM: *(Calling off)*
I'm not the one who just broke all the crockery.
Victor? Am I horrid?

VICTOR: *(Off)*
Specifically? Or in general?

JUSTINE: Ah—the worm turns.

WILLIAM: He does not. What worm?

(*A nervous* ELIZABETH *enters, followed by* VICTOR, *who loosens his shirt, against the oppressive heat of the day.*)

ELIZABETH: Weren't we going to the bank of the stream?

VICTOR: Yes, onward! It'd be so much cooler—

WILLIAM: But here in this meadow—see?
There are toadstools everywhere.
Justine felt at home.

JUSTINE: Now I'm an old maid *and* a witch?

WILLIAM: Then she put the hamper down—like this.
(He gives the basket a thump, so the others can hear the broken dishes.)

VICTOR: If Justine is a necromancer,
is it wise to be tattling?
She could find a mandrake-root,
and carve it into a tiny likeness of you—

WILLIAM: Oh, tosh! *You* don't believe in magic.
"It's only laws of nature
that ignorant people don't understand."

VICTOR: Explain one word of what you just said.

JUSTINE: He can't—he's a little parrot.

WILLIAM: I am! And I'll fly so far away,
you'll both be very sorry.

(WILLIAM *runs off, flapping his arms like wings.*)

VICTOR: *(Calling after him)*
Oh yes, we'll shed great crocodile tears.

(ELIZABETH *starts to follow* WILLIAM *off—then stops, unnerved.*)

VICTOR: Elizabeth? Is something wrong?

ELIZABETH: Do you smell it?
Something dead, in the woods.

(JUSTINE, *uneasy, remembers that smell.*)

JUSTINE: *(To* VICTOR*)*
Friend of yours, perhaps?

VICTOR: *(To* JUSTINE*)*
You forget your place, if you ever knew it.

(*But* VICTOR *is also nervous, and suddenly wants to find his brother.*)

VICTOR: Willie? Would you like to build a dam?
Willie, where are you?

(VICTOR *hurries off. As* JUSTINE *picks up the picnic-hamper,* ELIZABETH *speaks to her, quietly urgent.*)   .

ELIZABETH: Justine...

(JUSTINE *stops.*)

ELIZABETH: What was it like?

JUSTINE: *(Knowing very well)*
I don't know what you mean.

ELIZABETH: His hand on you.

(JUSTINE *doesn't respond.* ELIZABETH *forces herself to go on.*)

ELIZABETH: That day in the cellar—
Victor made advances...

JUSTINE: Months ago—and nothing happened.

ELIZABETH: Then why did you run from him?—
as if the very devil were after you?

(JUSTINE *puts down the basket again.*)

JUSTINE: All right:
his hand was cold—
the one he put over my mouth
when he bent me over.
Bone-cold, and rough—

ELIZABETH: *(Beginning to doubt)*
Victor's skin is smooth—

JUSTINE:—and rank, like a gutted animal—

ELIZABETH: He didn't—bend you over.

JUSTINE: No—I did that on my own.
I reached behind me
and spread myself wide open,
like a mouth.
Could you hear the words of my wet mouth?—
when I cried out: "I WANT!"

(Pause)

ELIZABETH: What has Victor done to you,
if he hasn't touched you? Tell me. Please.

(JUSTINE *doesn't answer.* ELIZABETH *suddenly grabs her.*)

ELIZABETH: There was something down there, in the
dark—
I know the smell of blood.
What was it?

JUSTINE: What do you think? A monster.
And it was very beautiful.

(ELIZABETH *stares at* JUSTINE, *trying to guess if she's telling
the truth. Then she hurries off, unable to look at* VICTOR.)

ELIZABETH: *(Off, calling out)*
William? Willie!

*(*JUSTINE *watches her go, half-heartedly taking up the cry.)*

JUSTINE: *(Calling out)*
Come out, come out, wherever you are!
(To herself:)
Or stay in your hidey-hole and rot.
(Calling out:)
You little monkey—we're tired!
Your cousin wants her tea!
I want—...
(She wonders what it is she wants.)
—to do nothing.
Would that be possible?
For a day or two, a week—
if I could simply—not move—

ELIZABETH: *(Off)* Justine? Is Willie there with you?

JUSTINE: No!

ELIZABETH: *(Off)* Then I'm going down to the river!
(Calling:)
Willy!

JUSTINE: I'll meet you!

ELIZABETH: *(Off)* Hurry!

JUSTINE: *(Not hurrying)*
I'm racing.

(As JUSTINE *starts to move off, her exit is suddenly blocked by the* CREATURE. JUSTINE *takes a step backward.)*

CREATURE: Justine.

JUSTINE: *(Terrified)*
Hello.
How have you been?
Where have you been?
I thought I dreamed you.

CREATURE: No.
You can feel my heart.
(Grabbing her hand)
Feel my heart!

(He presses her hand to his heart.)

CREATURE: Steady, strong...
I want it to stop.
Make it stop.
Kill me.
You said you would.

(With all her strength, JUSTINE pulls away from him, staggers back and falls. He leans over her.)

CREATURE: *Kill me.*

JUSTINE: I can't...

(Suddenly, far off, we hear ELIZABETH scream.)

ELIZABETH: *(Off)* VICTOR!

JUSTINE: *(To the CREATURE)*
My god, what have you done?
William...
(Crying out:)
WILLIAM!

*(The CREATURE strikes her. JUSTINE lies still.
The CREATURE feels her pulse.)*

CREATURE: *(Softly)*
Boom, boom, boom, boom...
Alive. Good.

(The CREATURE takes out the ring he stripped off WILLIAM's body. He slips it onto one of JUSTINE's fingers.)

CREATURE: Your little master had a gold ring.
You wanted it. He wouldn't give it to you.

(ELIZABETH runs on, in another part of the meadow.)

ELIZABETH: HELP ME! SOMEBODY HELP ME!

(As past and present merge, VICTOR—*followed by* WALTON—*runs on, only to halt—paralyzed, appalled by what he's remembering:* ELIZABETH *in agony, waiting for help...and the* CREATURE *hovering over* JUSTINE.*)*

VICTOR: *(To* WALTON, *of* ELIZABETH's *cries)* But it was too late for that.

(The CREATURE *stares at the unconscious* JUSTINE.*)*

CREATURE: *(To* JUSTINE*)*
Who made you?
God made you.
(Pause)
Where has He gone?

(The Arctic wind picks up.)

END OF ACT ONE

ACT TWO

Scene One

(JUSTINE's *cell. She's just told her story to* VICTOR.)

VICTOR: Where is the Creature now?

JUSTINE: I'd guess—in hiding,
till tomorrow night.
And then, from the shadows, it will watch me hang.
I die at midnight.

VICTOR: Why didn't you tell the authorities the truth?

JUSTINE: That "it wasn't *me*, Your Worship—
it was an 'orrible monster" ?

VICTOR: I can corroborate your story.

JUSTINE: And if they ask for proof?
(*Pause*)
You dismantled your laboratory,
I would imagine you burned your notes—

(VICTOR *did—he flinches.*)

JUSTINE:—the Creature is gone, a child is dead,
and I was the one they found
with a stolen ring on her bloody finger.

(*Pause*)

VICTOR: Do you think my brother suffered?

JUSTINE: Yes. I'm certain.
The Creature wants company.
He also wants an answer to his question.

VICTOR: What are you talking about?

JUSTINE: When he saw me stirring—after he hit me—
he bent down close, and he asked me:
"Why am I alive?"
I couldn't tell him.
He smiled.
You could have given him better teeth.

(A distant bell begins to toll the hour. ELIZABETH *and* VICTOR's FATHER *enter, approaching* JUSTINE's *cell—unnoticed at first.)*

JUSTINE: I never knew myself, why I was here—
and that would trouble me.
But by tomorrow night, I will never
have to wonder again.

VICTOR: Where do you think the Creature will hide,
until then?

JUSTINE: You won't find him.

VICTOR: Up in the mountains?

JUSTINE: I think you should leave me alone, now.
Guard!

*(*VICTOR's FATHER *now approaches.)*

FATHER: Victor? Get away from her!
That woman is a demon.

*(*VICTOR, *startled, spins around.)*

VICTOR: Papa!

FATHER: I forbade you to come here.

VICTOR: Justine isn't a murderess.

FATHER: Your mother bore nine children.
She has lost every one of them but you.
Now she's turning into a demon herself—

ELIZABETH: *(Trying to calm)*
Uncle...

VICTOR: Papa? What?

FATHER: Your mother won't give up the body.
See the scratches on my face?
She tore at me, when I tried to take it away.
She hasn't eaten, or slept. She rocks your little brother in her arms,
she sings him lullabies...

ELIZABETH: Victor, if you could talk to her...

(VICTOR looks back at JUSTINE, whose time is running out.)

VICTOR: I will. But when I return.
I have to go away.

FATHER: Now?

VICTOR: Up into the mountains.
Tell my mother I will be home by sunset.

ELIZABETH: Victor, why are you doing this?

(VICTOR puts his hands to ELIZABETH's face.)

VICTOR: Can you feel that?

ELIZABETH: What?

VICTOR: My brother's blood, still wet on my hands.
And you can pretend it isn't there—
let it dry and flake away, like rust—
but Justine is innocent, and
if I let her die—
my hands will be so slick with gore,
I will never be able to hold you.

(Desperate, VICTOR rushes out.)

FATHER: Victor? VICTOR!

(But VICTOR *is gone.)*

Scene Two

(In the mountains. VICTOR, *alone, is searching for the* CREATURE.*)*

VICTOR: WHERE ARE YOU?
WHY ARE YOU HIDING FROM ME?
I KNOW YOU'RE HERE—I CAN SMELL YOU!
EVERY PART OF YOU, ROTTING FLESH FALLING OFF OF
BLACK GUMS AND FESTERING BONES,
AND THE STENCH OF MY BROTHER'S BLOOD...

(The CREATURE *appears, behind* VICTOR.*)*

CREATURE: Shall I tell you how he died?

*(*VICTOR *can't bring himself to turn around.)*

VICTOR: No.

CREATURE: *(Relentless)*
This is how he died.

Scene Three

(By a stream. WILLIAM *enters, looking down into the water. Unnoticed, the* CREATURE *appears behind him, watching him.)*

WILLIAM: *(Calling off)*
Justine! Come and look at me in the water.
I don't have fingers—see?
(Checks his reflection, as he waves his fingers about)
I have big long feathers, beating the air
till I'm so high up,

the trees are little green puffs
and you people are specks,
you and Lizzie and Victor:
(Imitating)" Willy, come down!"—
But I *won't* come down—

(The CREATURE *approaches.* WILLIAM *sees its reflection
beside his own, in the water. Startled but not afraid,*
WILLIAM *turns to face the* CREATURE.)

WILLIAM: What happened to you?

CREATURE: I was dead.

WILLIAM: Oh.
(Pause)
I don't believe in ghosts.
Not in the daytime.
Are you hungry?

(The CREATURE *nods.)*

WILLIAM: I think we have cold chicken,
if you don't mind
the odd bit of broken plate—
Justine let the hamper drop.

CREATURE: "Justine..."

WILLIAM: Do you know her?

CREATURE: *(Dimly remembering)*
I was in pain—she could see that.
I said, "Help me."
She ran away.

WILLIAM: Yes, that would be Justine.
Where on earth did you meet her?

CREATURE: I don't remember.

WILLIAM: Maybe you hit your head.
Have you been attacked?
Is that what happened to you?

CREATURE: If I show my face—if they see me—
they shout at me, they throw rocks at me—
they beat me.
I live in the woods.

WILLIAM: But what do you eat?

CREATURE: What I can find:
roots, acorns, berries.

WILLIAM: And in the winter—where do you go?

CREATURE: *(Almost patient)*
Where do I go?
I live in the woods.

WILLIAM: But everything is dead.

CREATURE: Except for me. And I want to be still,
like the rest of the world,
but my heart keeps beating: "boom, boom..."
I lie awake all night,
with a rat in my stomach
trying to claw its way out,
and the wind is so cold,
sometimes I let the snow cover me over—
"this is my shroud."
But it isn't.
I always rise again, so I can suffer one more day.

WILLIAM: "Man was born to suffering."

CREATURE: Which man?

WILLIAM: I don't know. It's in the Bible.
Mother reads it to me when I've been bad:
I can quote whole passages.
Victor says it's rubbish,
but Mother says that's why she likes it,—
God seems to hate almost everyone,
and Mother is sympathetic.

CREATURE: "Victor"?

WILLIAM: My brother—Victor Frankenstein.
He's a doctor. He could help you.

CREATURE: Where does he work? In a cellar?

WILLIAM: How did you know that?

CREATURE: I was born there.

(WILLIAM *is finally frightened—he thinks the* CREATURE *is mad. He turns to run, but the* CREATURE *suddenly grabs him by the throat.*)

CREATURE: Your brother tortured me to life—
and then left me out on a hillside.
He thought I would starve,
or animals would attack me,
or winter would end me.
He didn't know how well he made me.
I am about to show him.

(WILLIAM, *terrified, tries to be brave.*)

WILLIAM: You're hurting me.

CREATURE: Am I?

WILLIAM: Please—let me go.

CREATURE: Does your brother love you?
Does he?

(WILLIAM *is afraid to answer "yes".*)

CREATURE: Maybe he can give birth to you,
when you're dead.
You and I can be brothers.
You can teach me how to pray.

(WILLIAM *tries to oblige.*)

WILLIAM: "The Lord is my shepherd—
I shall not want...."

CREATURE: Go on.

WILLIAM: "He leadeth me beside the still waters...
he restoreth my soul..."

CREATURE: I don't know what that is: "the soul".
Do you?

WILLIAM: I think it's rubbish.
A worm crawls out of the socket
where your eye had been. That's all.

(*Nodding agreement, the* CREATURE *strangles* WILLIAM.)

CREATURE: Can your brother not know that you
worship him?

(WILLIAM's *struggle is feeble and brief.*)

CREATURE: How can he help but love you?

(*The boy is dead. The* CREATURE *eases the body to the
ground.*)

CREATURE: But I will have my own disciples.
(*Pointing at the body:*)
SEE WHAT I HAVE CREATED!

(*Noticing a ring on* WILLIAM's *hand, the* CREATURE *bends
down and wrenches it off the finger.*)

CREATURE: ...and how I accept your offering.

Scene Four

(*In the mountains. Back with the* CREATURE, *who's finished
his story.* WILLIAM *is gone.* VICTOR *is disgusted by the*
CREATURE *and by himself.*)

VICTOR: Get out of my sight.

(*The* CREATURE *approaches* VICTOR, *who stands his ground,
afraid he's about to be killed.*)

CREATURE: All right—

(The CREATURE *reaches out and covers* VICTOR's *eyes with his frightening hands.)*

CREATURE: —I am gone.
Do you like it there, in the dark?
Alone? Pretending I don't exist?
(Removing his hands)
"Light."
(He covers VICTOR's *eyes again.)*
"Dark."

*(*VICTOR *thrusts the* CREATURE's *hands away from his face.)*

CREATURE: "Day."

(Staring at the CREATURE, VICTOR *shakes his head.)*

VICTOR: Night.
(Pause)
You speak very well.

CREATURE: I remembered letters—words—
from...whatever I was, before.
I had little enough to do in the woods,
so I set about improving myself.
I stole a few books—the Bible, *Paradise Lost*—
and I taught myself to read.
I thought there might be an answer...

VICTOR: To what question?

CREATURE: Why did you abandon me?

(Pause)

VICTOR: I wanted to save the world from death—
but all I gave you was life, and I saw that I had saved
you from nothing:
hunger, thirst, longing,
terrible loneliness like a cancer—

CREATURE: You mean you had made me human.

VICTOR: And I had hoped for something better.

CREATURE: Why didn't you simply destroy me?

(VICTOR *pulls out a dagger, being careful not to let the* CREATURE *see it.*)

VICTOR: Can you be destroyed?

(*Without warning,* VICTOR *suddenly plunges the dagger into the Creature's heart. The* CREATURE *stumbles and falls to the ground. He shudders, and is still.* VICTOR *stares at the body, appalled and elated by what he's done. Desperate to exonerate* JUSTINE, *he stumbles off. A moment later, the* CREATURE *opens his eyes. The horror of being alive rushes back. He screams. Crawling on his knees, he looks about him. He starts to weep.*)

Scene Five

(JUSTINE'*s cell.* JUSTINE *stares through the bars of her window.* VICTOR *enters.*)

VICTOR: Justine, I have been to the judge—
I told him everything.

JUSTINE: Did he believe you?

VICTOR: He called me a lunatic. "Sir, I am not disputing that," I replied, "but I have proof of my claim—"

JUSTINE: What proof?

VICTOR: The creature's body.

(*Despite her despair,* JUSTINE *is surprised.*)

VICTOR: I went up into the mountains
and I found it. And I killed it.

(CLERVAL *appears in the doorway of the cell.*)

CLERVAL: Victor?

VICTOR: What is it, Clerval?

CLERVAL: I've come to take you home.

VICTOR: I don't think they will let you.
Justine is innocent. I have confessed to the crime—

CLERVAL: You have a brain-fever.

VICTOR: *(Alarmed by* CLERVAL's *tone)*
No—my mind has never been clearer—

CLERVAL: Then why did you lie to the judge?
You babbled on, he said, about a
corpse you had—animated—

VICTOR: Yes—and then, too late, returned to the dust—

CLERVAL: Then where is the body?

*(*VICTOR *stares at* CLERVAL, *uncomprehending.)*

CLERVAL: The bailiff's men have searched the
mountainside—
and I accompanied them.

VICTOR: *(More and more afraid)* Near the timberline—
at the base of a cliff—

CLERVAL: And spreading out, far beyond it:
we looked everywhere.

VICTOR: *(Dreading the answer)*
And found nothing?

CLERVAL: What was there to find?

(Pause)

VICTOR: You truly believe I'm insane.

CLERVAL: No. I think grief has overcome you.

*(*JUSTINE *edges into hysteria.)*

JUSTINE: Yes, and me as well—
so I went on a rampage: "grief overcame me".

(She starts to laugh—it's frightening. VICTOR *grabs her.)*

VICTOR: YOU DIDN'T KILL MY BROTHER!

JUSTINE: Then why did I have his ring on my finger?
(*Pause*)
I would have pawned the ring,
and taken the money and run away.
(*Pause*)
I didn't want to be a servant the rest of my life,
but I had no savings.
And what else could I have been?
A fish-wife? A ladies' companion? A trollop?
I was trapped, and I thought that I could escape.
But first I needed capital:
so I killed a child.

VICTOR: YOU DIDN'T! THAT WAS THE ACT OF MY
CREATURE!

(*Pause*)

JUSTINE: What creature?

(VICTOR *stares at her, not knowing how he can prove his
guilt.*)

Scene Six

(*At the back door of* VICTOR'*s home.* ELIZABETH *enters,
with a lit candle. She peers out into the dark, afraid.*
VICTOR *enters.*)

VICTOR: Elizabeth?

ELIZABETH: Something is out there.

(*Pause*)

VICTOR: It doesn't want you.
Go back to bed.

(*Pause*)

ELIZABETH: Clerval said you were hallucinating.

VICTOR: No. You hear it yourself, in the garden,
just beyond the candlelight.

(*Pause*)

ELIZABETH: Do you still want to marry me?

VICTOR: You don't know what I've done.

(*Pause*)

ELIZABETH: I know you've always been afraid to love
me.

(*He doesn't answer.*)

ELIZABETH: Because I can die?
(*Pause*)
Because I'm already older now than I was
a second ago? And closer now to the time
when my flesh will sag, my eyes will cloud over...
I'll sit at the table, gumming my porridge,
forgetting the word I wanted, farting—
till even the dogs by the fire trot off in dismay:
how could you love me?

(*A bell begins to toll the hour.*)

VICTOR: Midnight.
Then Justine is dead.

(VICTOR *listens, haunted, till the sound of the bell fades
away. Overwhelmed by guilt, he finally tries to confess.*)

VICTOR: I will tell you what I did:
I had a child.
You were right to be frightened.
(*Pause*)
It quickened—I felt it stirring in me—
and then it tore me open.

ELIZABETH: (*Putting things together*)
In the cellar.

VICTOR: Yes.

ELIZABETH: A year ago.

(He nods.)

ELIZABETH: It isn't in the cellar now.

VICTOR: I abandoned it. Somehow it survived.

ELIZABETH: And in all that time—where has it been?

VICTOR: Out there. Waiting...

ELIZABETH: For what?

VICTOR: I don't know.
But it finally sought me out.
In terrible pain—

ELIZABETH: *(From experience)*
Because of its solitude.

(VICTOR begins to see how completely he misunderstood.)

VICTOR: I thought it was asking for something else—
to be put out of its misery.
I tried to kill it—
I thought I had.
But the body has disappeared.

ELIZABETH: No—it is right out there. Waiting...

VICTOR: To butcher anyone I love.

ELIZABETH: Ah. Well, then—at least *I'm* safe...

*(In desperate protest, VICTOR grabs ELIZABETH.
He kisses her, with shocking force. She struggles to
escape him. Finally she goes limp—and VICTOR is
overcome with shame. He lets her go; she trembles.)*

ELIZABETH: Find it. Bring it back to the house.

VICTOR: Are you mad? It killed my brother.
And an innocent woman hanged for the crime.

ELIZABETH: Then bring the creature home
before it claims another victim.

VICTOR: It will hide from me....

ELIZABETH: Then give up your pursuit.
What if we set a kind of trap?
Wouldn't it delight in being
the Uninvited Guest?

VICTOR: At a party?

ELIZABETH: At our wedding.

Scene Seven

*(In the mountains. VICTOR—with a skeptical CLERVAL—
is tracking the CREATURE. The offstage DOGS are barking in
confusion.)*

VICTOR: The dogs have lost the scent.

CLERVAL: It was here?

VICTOR: I stabbed him. He fell—by that rock.

CLERVAL: Victor, I helped to search this area.
We found nothing at all.
(Pause)
I was in the lead. I came upon
this clearing—and I was startled.
Because I had never been up here—
but this was the place I dreamed about.
Do you remember me telling you?
With a deep black pool, at the foot of a cliff.
You wanted to go for a swim, but I was afraid—

VICTOR: And then I kissed you.

(VICTOR approaches CLERVAL.)
What are you afraid of, now?

CLERVAL: You. The dream you had and won't let go of.

VICTOR: It isn't a dream!
(Pause)
Did you ever want to have a child, Clerval?

CLERVAL: I wasn't sure I would need one.
There was always you.
(Pause)
Does Elizabeth believe in your creature?

VICTOR: She hopes it will come to our wedding—
that I might finally offer it shelter.
But if it does appear at our door,
I think it will want much more than that.

(CLERVAL begins to suspect the truth.)

CLERVAL: So you decided to hunt it down?

(VICTOR doesn't answer, but CLERVAL understands.)

CLERVAL: Or is it hunting us?

(VICTOR doesn't deny this.)

CLERVAL: Come back with me to the village.

(VICTOR tears himself away from CLERVAL's sympathy.)

VICTOR: No. *(He calls out to the unseen CREATURE.)*
I AM HERE! SHOW YOURSELF!

(VICTOR starts to run off—CLERVAL grabs him.)

CLERVAL: Victor—

VICTOR: Clerval, let go of me.

(CLERVAL lets go. VICTOR stares at him.)

VICTOR: Do you understand? Forever: let go.
(He suddenly dashes off, calling out again.)
WHERE ARE YOU? WHERE?

CLERVAL: *(Shouting after him)*
Your mind is unbalanced!
Victor—let me help you!

(CLERVAL *starts to run off—and almost collides with the*
CREATURE, *whom he has never seen and never completely*
believed in. CLERVAL *recoils, then tries to hide his fear.*
The CREATURE, *who has spied on* VICTOR's *family,*
recognizes CLERVAL.)

CREATURE: Why did he give me a cock?

CLERVAL: I don't know.
So you can make little monsters?
I couldn't begin to guess—
do you use it to urinate?
I don't know.
(*Pause*)

CREATURE: Did he ever love you?

CLERVAL: Perhaps...
All he cares about now is you.

(*Pause*)

CREATURE: When I killed his little brother—
when I made them hang the serving-girl—
my cock got hard. It was like a club.
Why have I got a cock?
(*Pause*)
Tell him I need a wife.

CLERVAL: I didn't understand you could simply
order a mate from his workshop.

(*The* CREATURE *comes nearer.*)

CREATURE: Someone to hold me, late at night,
when the rain comes down and puts out the fire....
Call him to me. Now.

(CLERVAL, *deeply frightened, shakes his head.*)

CREATURE: I know how to propose—I was in the
shadows, watching him.
He taught me.

(Pause)

(As VICTOR *grabbed* ELIZABETH, *the* CREATURE *suddenly grabs* CLERVAL. *He kisses him, with ferocity.* CLERVAL *fights to get away, but the* CREATURE *holds him by the neck.)*

CREATURE: I want a wife.

CLERVAL: And after he made you one—
a virgin-fiend—
would you let him live?

(The CREATURE *throws* CLERVAL *to the ground.)*

CREATURE: If you scream, will he come to your rescue?

CLERVAL: No.

(The CREATURE *suddenly hits* CLERVAL, *who cries out, before he can stop himself.)*

VICTOR: *(Off)* Clerval?

CREATURE: You were lying. Scream again.

(He hits CLERVAL *again—but* CLERVAL *is able to stifle his cry.)*

CREATURE: Cry for help—or you are a dead man.

*(*CLERVAL *crawls away from his attacker, dragging himself offstage. The* CREATURE *exits, pursuing him, grimly deliberate.* VICTOR *enters, looking around.)*

VICTOR: Clerval, I heard voices—where are you?
(Suddenly he is very afraid.)
CLERVAL?

(The CREATURE *enters.)*

CREATURE: I asked him to give you a message.
But he refused.

VICTOR: What did you do to him?

(The CREATURE *doesn't answer.)*

VICTOR: CLERVAL!

CREATURE: He cannot hear you.

(VICTOR *slumps, devastated.*)

VICTOR: I am the one who harmed you.
Why are you slaughtering innocent people—
one after another—man, woman and child?

CREATURE: So you will do my bidding.

VICTOR: And if I refuse?

CREATURE: I can always spare you.
And watch your conscience devour you.

VICTOR: I will kill myself.

CREATURE: You don't have the courage.
Isn't that why you sought me out?
(*Pause*)
You are getting married.

VICTOR: Yes.

CREATURE: I would like a wife as well.
Make me one.

VICTOR: You can rot in hell.

CREATURE: I am already rotting. Here on earth.
(*Pause*)
I am alone, because your kind
will not associate with me.
But if you brought to life a woman
as horrible and deformed as myself,
she would accept me, and
we would disappear into the wild forever.

VICTOR: Or the two of you could band together
to desolate the world.

CREATURE: If I had the love of another,
why would I need to avenge myself?

VICTOR: It took me almost a year to make you.
Can you wait that long?

CREATURE: No.

VICTOR: I had to assemble you, part by part—

CREATURE: Why? Dig up a single body.
One that has only begun to cool.
Justine.

VICTOR: *(Horrified)*
No...

(Offstage, the DOGS *begin to howl.)*

CREATURE: The dogs have found your friend.

(Pause)

VICTOR: Where is he now?
You said it was night...

CREATURE: Without end. Forever and ever.

VICTOR: Cold?

(The CREATURE *doesn't answer.)*

VICTOR: Peaceful?

CREATURE: Nothing.

VICTOR: And you were alone.

CREATURE: Completely.

VICTOR: Was that agony?

CREATURE: It was nothing.

(Pause)

VICTOR: Then why is it agony now?

(Pause)

CREATURE: Maybe Justine can tell you.

VICTOR: *(Still fighting this demand)*
No.
Let the woman sleep.

CREATURE: Is she asleep?
Then she must have been buried alive.
Dig her up.

VICTOR: I will not do it.

(VICTOR forces himself to turn his back on the CREATURE, dreading its anger, and stumbles away. The CREATURE stares after him. He smiles a terrible smile.)

Scene Eight

(VICTOR's home. ELIZABETH is comforting Victor's FATHER, who is weeping. VICTOR rushes in.)

VICTOR: That man in the hall—

FATHER:—is the undertaker.

VICTOR: *(Aware of this)*
Send him away. GET RID OF HIM!

(VICTOR's outburst is shocking. No-one moves.)

VICTOR: My mother is dead. When?

FATHER: Do you care? An hour ago.
Victor, where have you been?

VICTOR: Was she strangled?
Was she torn apart?

FATHER: She died of a broken heart. In her sleep.
Your brother's death was too much for her.
She might have turned to you for consolation.
But you were gone.

VICTOR: Did she ask for me? What were her final words?

FATHER: She said, "Where is the cat?"
And then she said, "Where is Victor?
I wanted to say goodbye".

(VICTOR *speaks, from ghoulish experience.*)

VICTOR: Your undertaker drinks too much.
At the end of the day, when he staggers off,
he forgets to lock his doors.
So vandals wander into his charnel-house,
and desecrate the bodies.
They take souvenirs.

ELIZABETH: Don't speak of these things.

VICTOR: A finger, if the ring is stuck—
a glass eye someone could sell again,
a tooth with a golden filling—

ELIZABETH: Stop it!

VICTOR: Smash the jaw with a crow-bar—

FATHER: Victor—why do you hurt us this way?
Why are you hurting yourself?
Your mother loved you.

VICTOR: Then I should have saved her.
I didn't.
(*He stares at his* FATHER *and* ELIZABETH.)
And now I may have waited too long to save you...

(*Without another word,* VICTOR *dashes off.*
VICTOR's FATHER *and* ELIZABETH, *deeply upset,*
watch VICTOR *go.*)

Scene Nine

(The graveyard. In a thunderstorm. VICTOR enters, pushing
a laden wheelbarrow. Tied to one of the handles is the string
of a kite stretching taut into the dark sky. JUSTINE's body
lies in the barrow, hidden by a tarpaulin. One of her arms
dangles over the side, uncovered, wet and gleaming.
VICTOR wheels the barrow into place. Then he takes in
the storm—lightning-flash, almost simultaneous crash
of thunder.)

VICTOR: I have a power no murderer ever had:
I can give you back what I stole from you.
(Pause)
But do you want it?
(Pause)
Justine, where are you now?
Up above, playing airs on a little harp?
Or below, in a lake of fire, dragging
your burning body to shore?
Or was my Creature telling the truth?
Is there nothing at all—
and are you content?

(Another dazzle of lightning, clap of thunder.
VICTOR looks around, expecting to see the CREATURE.)

VICTOR: He is in this graveyard, now—he must be:
hating me for giving him life—
but waiting for me to commit the same crime against
you.
And if I falter...
I know he will slaughter Elizabeth,
and drop her broken body at my feet—
that will be his wedding gift.
(Pause. To JUSTINE:)

Then you have to be mine, to him.
Forgive me, Justine.

(He begins to wrap the cord of the kite around the dangling hand of JUSTINE. *The wind picks up. The kite flies higher, tugging* JUSTINE's *hand and arm up into the air. A lightning-bolt hits the kite. As thunder booms, the kite-string glows.* JUSTINE *sits up in the wheelbarrow, shedding the tarpaulin that had covered her. Arm still held aloft by the kite,* JUSTINE *stares out—a look of horror on her face.)*

JUSTINE: I want—...

VICTOR: What? Tell me!

(She sags.)

JUSTINE: I want—to go—

VICTOR: Where?

JUSTINE: Home. *(Another lightning-bolt hits the kite.* JUSTINE *rises up, more nearly alive.)* I WANT!

VICTOR: Where is home?

JUSTINE: THE DARK—FOREVER.

VICTOR: *(Already regretting what he's done)* Can you find the way?

JUSTINE: I CAN SEE IT—
BACK THROUGH A DOOR,
OH LET ME, PLEASE—
THE DARK, FOREVER AND EVER—
WHY AM I CAUGHT IN THIS NET,
WILL SOMEBODY CUT THE,
SET ME FREE! THE CORD!
I WANT!
I WANT!—

*(*JUSTINE *falters again, not quite alive.* VICTOR, *making a sudden decision, grabs the string of the kite and starts to work it free from* JUSTINE's *hand.)*

VICTOR: Go back, then.

CREATURE: *(Offstage)* NO!

(VICTOR flinches, but only works faster.)

VICTOR: Go back to the dark.

(The CREATURE rushes in. He wrestles with VICTOR, who jerks the final loop of string from JUSTINE's hand. JUSTINE crumples. As creator and creation fight for the kite, it is hit by lightning one more time. Both the CREATURE and VICTOR stagger from the shock. In that moment, VICTOR wrenches himself from the CREATURE's grip, and—very deliberately—lets go of the kite-string. The CREATURE watches it soar into the night-sky and disappear. Exhausted, VICTOR sinks to his knees. The CREATURE, desolate, moves to JUSTINE, putting his hand to her neck, to feel for a pulse.)

CREATURE: Nothing.
Nothing.
NOTHING!
I WANTED—...

(Pause)

VICTOR:—not to want anymore.

(The CREATURE stares at VICTOR.)

CREATURE: I am going.

VICTOR: Where?

CREATURE: Does it matter?
I will be with you
on your wedding-night.

(The CREATURE moves off, leaving VICTOR alone with JUSTINE's body.)

Scene Ten

(On the iceberg. VICTOR *has almost finished his story.)*

WALTON: You didn't believe him...

VICTOR: Yes—I did.

WALTON: Then you gave up any hope of ever marrying
Elizabeth?

(Not answering, VICTOR *points off, toward the horizon.)*

VICTOR: Your ship would be—there?

(Intent on VICTOR's *story,* WALTON *barely looks up.)*

WALTON: You can make out the sails,
catching the final light.

VICTOR: And the figures on the ice?
That pitiful band—are they your men?

(Alerted, WALTON *stares out.)*

WALTON: Where? *(He sees.)*
God help them—have they all gone mad?
Do they think they can *walk* to Sevastapol?

(Suddenly FORSTER *clambers up onto the ice.)*

FORSTER: Captain Walton!

VICTOR: *(Astonished, to* FORSTER*)*
Who the devil are you?

WALTON: My lieutenant. Or he was, before.
Have you also joined the mutiny?

FORSTER: Sir, an hour ago the open water
finally closed astern.
The trap has shut.
I gave the men the order to abandon ship.

(WALTON is stunned—but also aware of his own dereliction of duty.)

WALTON: You took command.

FORSTER: In your absence.
Not being certain of your return. Sir.

WALTON: I could bring you up on charges.

FORSTER: *(A challenge)*
If we make it back to land.

(Reluctantly, WALTON begins to make a decision.)

WALTON: Is the crew unloading supplies?

FORSTER: Yes sir.

WALTON: Tell them to set aside provisions enough
for a week—
(Indicating VICTOR)
—for this man.

FORSTER: Why?

WALTON: Because I am leaving him here—
under so many stars, he will never
count them all.

FORSTER: *(Unwilling to waste supplies)*
Hard for him to count,
when he's dead as a door-nail—
begging your pardon, sir.
He won't come with us?

VICTOR: No.

WALTON: *(Dismissing FORSTER)*
I will meet you back at the ship.

FORSTER: Yes sir. We ought to move out—soon—
before the weather falls apart.

(FORSTER exits. WALTON turns to VICTOR.)

WALTON: Finish your story, and I will go.
What happened to Elizabeth?

(VICTOR *hesitates.*)

WALTON: Tell me, and I swear to you:
I can keep them alive, forever—
the people you never wanted to die—
I can say, "Once upon a time..."

Scene Eleven

(ELIZABETH *enters, in her nightgown, a candle lit in her hand.* VICTOR *stands, looking out at the night.*)

ELIZABETH: Victor? Is he out there?

VICTOR: I don't know, anymore.
He may be gone.
But he will come back—
on our wedding-night. He promised.

ELIZABETH: What if we marry in secret?

VICTOR: Somehow he would hear.

ELIZABETH: What if we marry now?

(ELIZABETH *lets her robe fall from her, revealing her nakedness.*)

VICTOR: Do you know how beautiful you are?
And how your beauty hurts?

(*Pause. He kneels in front of her, kissing her.
She strokes his hair.*)

ELIZABETH: Could that be how your Creature felt—
when he opened his eyes,
and he found himself back in the world?

(*Pause. Behind* VICTOR *and* ELIZABETH, *the* CREATURE *appears, listening.*)

ELIZABETH: That first winter had to be terrible.
But I wonder if the spring was worse—
to feel a warm breeze, or the sun on his skin—
look up, and all the new green glowing—
snow melting off into streams he could drink from,
cold, and clear as the sound of water
running over rocks, and the cries of birds,
and the smell of grass...

VICTOR: ...lie down on his back, and be still,
and know the whole wide world was trembling—
breathing in and out:
alive.
(*Pause*)
What could that beauty have been like—
to a thing so completely alone?

(ELIZABETH *gently moves from* VICTOR, *sensing that he
finally understands.*)

ELIZABETH: I am going to bed.
Come and marry me.

(VICTOR *hesitates, looking out at the night—wondering if
the* CREATURE *is there.*)

VICTOR: Let me be certain the doors and windows are
locked.

(ELIZABETH—*hoping* VICTOR *will follow her—moves off.
When she's almost out of sight, the* CREATURE *steps out of
the shadows, blocking her way.* VICTOR—*still looking for
danger outside—doesn't see this.* ELIZABETH *stares at the*
CREATURE—*knowing she's going to die. The lights change.*)

Scene Twelve

(VICTOR *ends his story.*)

VICTOR: She was lying on the bed, where he left her—
I thought, for a moment, that she was asleep.
But then I took a step closer,
and I saw that her mouth was open
in a scream that he had stifled...
How could I look at that and live?
(*Pause*)
Because, my creature taught me, life is obstinate—
and holds us tighter, when we hate it most.
(*Pause*)
Since that night, I have sought revenge.
And my pursuit has led me here.

(*Pause*)

WALTON: But—even if you found him—
you tried to kill him before...

VICTOR: And I failed.
I will have to destroy his body.
I brought a supply of lamp-oil.
I will douse him, and set him aflame.

(*Far off, the eerie sound of timber groaning.*
WALTON *looks out.*)

WALTON: My ship is breaking apart,
as the ice closes in.
(*Watches the* Aurora *starting to sink*)
My first command...

VICTOR: But not your last—if you can survive the trek.
(*Seeing* WALTON's *reluctance:*)
You aren't abandoning me:

you are saving your men.
Leading them home.

WALTON: *(Daunted)* A hundred miles from land.
How many will perish, on the way?
Because I thought that I was—
not the most impressive, but still—a God...

VICTOR: Perhaps you are, in this much:
that you can suffer with your men.

(The creaking of timber being crushed is louder.)

WALTON: If you die—what will become of the Creature?

(VICTOR can't bear to consider that.)

WALTON: It will live—and what then?

VICTOR: You can give a warning to the world.
If you will go.

(Accepting his duty, but desolate, WALTON exits. VICTOR watches him go. Then he opens one of his knapsacks, carefully laying out a flask of oil and a flint-and-steel, for making a spark. As he does this, the CREATURE appears.)

CREATURE: You want to burn me alive?

(VICTOR whirls about and sees the CREATURE approaching. Before he can move, the CREATURE is on him, knocking him to the ice. Then the CREATURE picks up the flask.)

CREATURE: What does that feel like, I wonder?
(Savagely, he splashes lamp-oil on VICTOR.)
One day, the winter you left me—
when the cold was like a whip,
and the tears were freezing on my cheeks—
I found a fire, still smouldering,
that some wandering beggars had left behind.
And the warm was such a relief,
I wanted to hold it in my hands.
I bent down, and picked up a glowing ember.
And screamed: could the fire be both at once?

Pleasure, and also unbearable pain?
Later I came to realize
that that was the nature of life.

(Putting the flask of oil aside, he strikes the block of steel with the flint, producing a shower of sparks. VICTOR scrambles away from the CREATURE, terrified of being ignited.)

CREATURE: Even so my revenge:
I destroyed your hopes,
but what was I left, of my own?
I still desire love—
and I am abominated forever.
(He stares at VICTOR.)
Stop cowering. Are you that afraid of dying?

VICTOR: Why do you think I made you?

CREATURE: But—if you aren't alone—
if I accompany you...

(The CREATURE picks up the oil again, now pouring it over himself. Knowing the CREATURE will be destroyed, VICTOR begins to accept his fate.)

VICTOR: So this will be my legacy:
two heaps of ash. And then
the wind will sweep them into the sea.
(Pause)
Will I have thoughts, in the darkness?
Will I dream?

CREATURE: Are you certain you want to?
Or is it not because of your dreams
that you and I are here?

(A loud splintering crash, and the crevice widens, separating VICTOR from the CREATURE.)

CREATURE: No!
NO!

(VICTOR watches the CREATURE, across the abyss.)

CREATURE: Come back. *(The* CREATURE *reaches out a hand.)* Come back!

*(*VICTOR *hesitates—but only a moment. Then he reaches out, to grab the outstretched hand.* VICTOR *jumps—and barely makes it across, as the* CREATURE *hauls him in. With a shudder, the ice where* VICTOR *had been drops into the dark. The wind picks up.* VICTOR *and the* CREATURE *regard each other. The* CREATURE *tries, a final time, to start a fire with flint-and-steel. A few glints—but they die in the wind.)*

CREATURE: The spark goes out.
Why does the spark go out?

*(*VICTOR *holds out his cupped hands, to make a wind-break. The* CREATURE, *understanding, strikes the flint behind the shelter of* VICTOR's *hands. A shower of sparks in the dark. Then—a second of blinding light: the* CREATURE *and* VICTOR, *blazing—)*

(Blackout)

END OF PLAY